The Distance Bet

By the author

Staring Directly at the Eclipse
Travelling Second Class Through Hope
Raining Upwards
Art By Johnny ★
A Normal Family •
This Phantom Breath
The Department of Lost Wishes
Swallowing the Entire Ocean
Strikingly Invisible
The Escape Plan
The Beauty Within Shadow
The Distance Between Clouds

★ Collated & edited by Henry Normal
• With Angela Pell & published by Two Roads

THE DISTANCE BETWEEN CLOUDS

Henry Normal

Flapjack Press
www.flapjackpress.co.uk

Exploring the synergy between performance and the page

Published in 2021 by Flapjack Press
Salford, Gtr Manchester
⊕ flapjackpress.co.uk
f Flapjack Press 🐦 FlapjackPress

ISBN 978-1-8381185-8-7

Cover art by Johnny Carroll-Pell
f Art By Johnny 📷 johnnycarrollpell

Front flap photo by Alun Callender
Back flap photo by Angela Pell

Printed by Imprint Digital
Exeter, Devon
⊕ digital.imprint.co.uk

FSC

MANCHESTER
A UNESCO City
of Literature

I would like to dedicate this book to Tony Hallam,
even though he will no doubt think the whole idea 'ridic'.

*I would like to thank Linda Hallam,
Paul Neads, Penny Shepherd and Angela Pell
for their help in bringing this collection together.*

Contents

Tuning out background noise   13

Things I wouldn't be seen dead in   14

The shyness of the crown   15

The pros and cons of publishing poetry   16
    i. Haikudos
    ii. If this page were still part of a tree

Low tide   17

Be individually wrapped   18

A long weight   20

The easing of restrictions   20

Birthday card delivered by Asda   20

Seaford seafront at Phase 3   21

Ten things they never tell you …   22

A second boat amid the storm   24

There are things you can't unknow   25

Homage to fromage   26

Life imitating art imitating life   28

Initial thoughts on name dropping   28

The imaginary invalid (sans encore)   29

Altogether unmemorable   29

A new memory to replace the one forgotten   30

Morning poem   32

Autumn sunset   32

These defences we build are still so paper thin   33

I may be giving up breathing for Lent   34

Ennui normal   35

Storm gathering   36

Coneflower   38

A hyacinth by another name would smell as sweet   38

In drawers that never open   39

Every nation is an immigrant nation   40

Forget the statue can we just play with the box?   40

Brutus's arrival in the land of Albina   41

The glorious revolution   41
British fashion found to be old school   41
The common denominator   42
My garden is probably past its best   43
Five a day I can do in four   44
A dog's life for a god   46
Lodestar   47
Corona nursery rhymes   48
The shrinking sky   50
Less hip, more hip replacement   51
Unavoidable neglect   52
You can take nothing from me …   53
All creatures great and small …   54
The sundial casts no shadow   55
Some days the only thing I like deep …   56
Maybe there is another universe …   58
Let us not bury those merely sleeping   59
I've no beef with tripe   60
The sun navigates a corridor between clouds   61
This poetry is   62
I'd sooner be a citizen than a subject   63
The five stages of good grief!   64
War mongers   65
Becoming conscious during Covid   66
Grounded   67
Those little slices of death   68
I am not the poet I longed to be   70
Whisper from a future grave   71
The secret of eternal youth   72
Chasing immortality   72
Forest poems   73
    i. The origin of Nottingham Forest's shirt colour
    ii. Nottingham – first English city of football
    iii. If blood is red why are veins blue?
    iv. Blue cheese for a red
In a world without God or fame   74

The invisible mantra	75
The unslept	76
Converting light into energy	77
1616	78
Constantine the Great (or not so)	78
Next door's cat is nowhere to be seen	79
Twitter poetry	80
Artificial trees	80
Ladders of divine ascent	81
An empty hallway awaiting new guests	82
The Earth is not a perfect circle	83
All eyes on the potato	84
The lure of the salmon sandwich	86
John Byrom	86
Byron trilogy	87
i. The folly of the Pena Palace, Sintra	
ii. Any old Ionian	
iii. Epitaph to a dog – Butch not Boatswain	
Less than temporary	88
What not to say to a poet	89
Catchy verse	90
Fly-solation	90
A martyr to my 'John the Baptist complex'	91
1189 – the first pub crawl	92
Nottingham centre trilogy	93
i. 1642 – a poem for GCSE syllabus	
ii. Cast irony	
iii. Is Helen elsewhere in Nottingham?	
A day off from social media	94
I'm not good at self-deprecation	95
The origin of Old Coach Road, Wollaton	96
Nottingham tram trilogy	97
i. Mad, bad and safe for passengers	
ii. She walks in beauty like the night tram	
iii. Loneliness of the long distance on runners	
It lives!	98

There are no peacocks beneath this tired sky 99
Good form 100
Acrostic poem 100
Fare thee well 101
The Christmas star in a time of darkness 102
The poetry unwritten 103
Teenagers didn't invent sex 104
The nearly famous 105
A tree with its own visitors' centre 106
Batman filmed at Wollaton Hall … 106
12,000 year old Frank 106
Fifteen ways to leave your lockdown 107
Responsibility wakes me 108
Higher stratus clouds above the channel 109
Shaking hands with Elvis 110
Boudica is a thing of the pasta 112
T' realism 112
Happy St. David's Day 112
Reclamation 113
Nottingham's son 114
It's 116
Folding 117
Stick or twist again like we didn't … 118
To the night 120
The eleventh month is named after … 121
F.O.P. (but not ready to drop) 122
The distance between clouds 124

The Distance Between Clouds

Tuning out background noise

When too many people
speak at once
it's difficult to make sense
of what is being said

When life comes at you
too fast
it can be hard
to understand how you feel

In the calm of a poem
you can gather thoughts
take time to breathe
and set out the world

on the page
in some form of order
so you can see it
more clearly

Things I wouldn't be seen dead in

I'll never wear a onesie
I'll never wear crocs
tank tops, flip flops
sandals with socks

If you see me wearing dungarees
kill me please
A puffa jacket is in that bracket

but a covering for my face is ace
and makes the chances greater, that later
someone won't be wearing a ventilator

The shyness of the crown

Channels of light
within the canopy

where trees leave space
for each other

especially those
in windswept forests

sensitive to shade
and touch

protecting themselves
and those close to

The pros and cons of publishing poetry

i. **Haikudos**

If I'd not written
this haiku we would not be
sharing this moment

ii. **If this page were still part of a tree**

it could offer shade
and take in your latest breath
to help make your next

Low tide

The floor of the English Channel
is exposed

My loved ones paddle barefoot
in puddles

All around toddlers and gulls
find a new balance

Further out to sea teenagers
dare themselves another step

Sailing ships and even speed boats
seem in no hurry today

There's a slight haze like spilt flour
on a blue table top

A man in shorts loses himself
with a net and bucket

Behind me white cliffs stretch out
open arms

Underfoot the chalk continues south
crowned by seaweed

The myth
of our island nation is revealed

We are, as ever, joined to each
continent by land

The water just sits on top
reflecting sunlight

all the way to the horizon

Be individually wrapped

Stay healthy – be a hermit
to help the old and infirm it
may be short term – yet to confirm it

Form your own exclusive club
snub the hub and don't forget to scrub
that's the nub

On a sabbatical be
emphatically
position yourself somewhat statically

Social contact is easily quit-able
stay home and become inhospitable
to any virus that's transmittable

Forget that outing – stick to inning
so all of us will end up winning
that's the logic underpinning

Prefer aversions to excursions
defer all unwarranted incursions
procure yourself some small diversions

Lay flat that 'unwelcome mat'
keep your hat to your own habitat
Zoom and Snapchat's where it's at

There's social media and Wikipedia
and parts of the internet a little seedier
to feed y' brain why don't you read yeah?

Enjoy self-isolation for the duration
join the nation on a grand staycation
get a separate room in a separate location

Put on the brake and take all your days off
fill your cake-hole full of stuff you can graze off
being Billy No-Mates finally pays off

A long weight

Dumbbells that arrived yesterday
delivered to my door
still sit there today
I can't lift them off the floor

The easing of restrictions

Sizeable queues at Primark
asking what they'd charge
to exchange 'medium' clothes
now needed in 'extra large'

Birthday card delivered by Asda

Happy Birthday to you
Squashed Tomatoes and Stew
I know you ordered Chopped Tomatoes
I hope this substitute will do

Seaford seafront at Phase 3

Hopefully I haven't killed anyone today
the family further down the beach
has backed off

Bathed in UV rays
restrictions easing
a chance to get away from it all

As a new group enters the sea
my son
swims east to avoid contact

We are not far from
the stainless steel fishes
with the names of the dead

An old couple
park themselves
too close upwind

My mind still alert
as the ferry sets sail
I think of tinned virus

Skin cancer takes second place
stones in the sand look like nodules
buoys – Covid marking out restrictions

A chubby child
in a spotted swimsuit
resembles Corona on legs

Ten things they never tell you about being a new parent

1.
You will sing everything you do with your baby
using the most obvious of rhymes
mostly in a voice like a female impersonator
or a daytime TV presenter

2.
You will keep a mental log
of your baby's bowel movements
output, consistency and colouration

3.
You will look at your child's face constantly
You will take too many photos
and find it hard to delete any

4.
You will prefer half an hour's sleep to sex
You will prefer half an hour's sleep to anything
You will prefer anything to sex

5.
You will want to kill your baby
lose it, hand it back
Whilst the next moment wanting to snog it
hug it, eat it and die for it

6.
You will take at least two hours
to get out of the house
and once you arrive at your destination
it will be time to get ready to leave

7.
You will look at every other baby
Talk to most
Judge them to be less perfect than your own

8.
You will walk around
with sick and piss and shit on your best clothes
unconcerned, whilst removing all sharp
or dangerous objects instinctively

9.
You will forgive your parents

10.
You will say the words 'He's my son'
or 'She's my daughter'
and reeling from the significance
you will lose your breath

A second boat amid the storm

A second boat amid the storm
shouldn't sail too close
waves are harsh enough
without a clash of bows

A second boat amid the storm
shouldn't drift in the dark
you may be their only salvation
they may be yours

There are things you can't unknow

Aware, I have a choice

I can sit staring
at the seagull shit
staining my window

or I can get up and wash it off

or I can realign my bench
and enjoy April
cajoling my garden to dance

understanding
the shit is still there
albeit out of sight

I'll try the last option for now

knowing only too soon
the sun will go in
and Ajax will come out

or rainfall will change everything

Homage to fromage *(mentions 26 cheeses so read Caerphilly)*

"Poets have been mysteriously silent on the subject of cheese."
– G.K. Chesterton

I'm thinking I'll dish up
some Stinking Bishop

and a chunk of Cheshire
– always a pleasure

I'm having an affair with Camembert
I'm more than a fan of Parmesan

For Mascarpone I've no acrimony
Edam I eat by the kilogram

On the goodness of Gouda
I couldn't shout louder

but Feta is better –
like giving your tastebuds a lactose love letter

Mozzarella is stellar
Emmental is no risk at all

With Wensleydale you can scarcely fail
You can add Double Gloucester to that roster

I've not forgot a – Fresh Ricotta
and often request a – Red Leicester

though a Kraft Cheese Slice
can oft' suffice

Maybe – I'll wangle some Brie
or a triangle of Dairylea

and what could be cooler
than a squirt of Primula?

Even Babybel goes down well
but Philadelphia is healthier

and, of course, Cheddar
there's nothing 'beddar'

Blue Vein – I might try again
although Halloumi is a lot less fumy

Stilton – an acquired taste that can be built on
still it gives you breath most flowers will wilt on

My curd-based tastes are fairly broad
I never get bored of the cheese board

but Gorgonzola
tastes like dairy Ebola

like being French-kissed by the dead Ayatollah
or your tongue run over by a septic steamroller

and Hell would need to freeze
before I eat Vegan Cheese

Life imitating art imitating life

My memory of the movie *Titanic*
and I'm sad to say it's true
folk waiting in the foyer causing a panic
with the selfish jumping the queue

Initial thoughts on name dropping

Ah yes W.H. Auden, T.S. Eliot
I'm on first name terms with every great poet
e.e., W.B. and WWW. we must not forget
he's very big on the internet

B.O.
not so popular though

The imaginary invalid (sans encore)

Moliere might have appreciated it
for irony he didn't lack
His cause of death – a coughing fit
playing a hypochondriac

Altogether unmemorable
(say critics of Tchaikovsky's new ballet in 1877)

Initially this one
failed to convince
though many a pen
has died since

With *Swan Lake*
it doesn't take
analytics

to calculate
the weight
of critics

A new memory to replace the one forgotten

There is a little old man
aged three
sitting on a doorstep
that doesn't exist

The inner edge
of the front door
is exposed
revealing wear

Chalk marks
on the wall
look like a robot
and a declaration of love

Prompted by the photo
my sister
still by my side
remembers this moment

Our living room
where we never lived
is too dark
to provide detail

My cousin
is perhaps as yet
unaware
that he's gay

My aunty smiles
at her husband-to-be
prior to sixty years
of marriage

It is eight years
until my mum dies
I don't recognise
myself

Morning poem

for Lemn Sissay

The dawn is red
then the sky is blue
the sun is playing
peekaboo

Autumn sunset

Twilight turns to dusk
sunlight burns to rust

These defences we build are still so paper thin

It is difficult to forgive
the worst in us
when we yearn so much
for the best

It is scary to see
how easily we fall
when we appear to have
climbed so high

It is heartbreaking
that for all our pain
there's no safe place
to rest

It is a reminder
of how far we've come
but how much harder
we have to try

I may be giving up breathing for Lent

Repenting the sin of gluttony
my cardigan now stretches
            near where it's buttony

Those pancakes were too buttery
the cholesterol sends my heart fluttery

Fat Tuesday
Stomach Abuse Day
I fret
        I'll regret
                this threat
                        utterly

Ennui normal

Boring – bears exploring
Insipid sends my soul a-soaring

Lethargy fills me with glee
Tedium is my cup of tea

An absence of umph
a veritable triumph

Prosaic is my Prozac
Predictable – my pure grade crack

Irksome can work some
Tiresome can inspire some

Listless – I couldn't resist less
Lifeless – my troubles exist less

Ponderous I find wondrous
Drab and dreary – fab and cheery

A lull is never dull
A lack of sparkle – sans debacle

Lacklustre – deserves all the energy I can muster
Jejune – floats my balloon

Mind numbing – I find becoming
A life unleaden – would be Armageddon

Who don't like samey – is cockamamie

Storm gathering

As pressure plummets
gulls know better than to fly

From beneath branches
they complain constantly

The wind has changed direction
and at last the air tastes fresh

Having worked almost a complete day
the sun settles down to rest

A pink haze flirts with the edge of clouds
The netting on my balcony twitches nervously

A single passenger plane escapes south
its engine a precursor to thunder

Sea fret joins the party
The horizon becomes sullen

A small red light speeds back to the marina
The coast road shushes a baby to sleep

The water darkens
A first rumble low in the gut

Some buzzing insect seeks refuge in my ear
before I bat it away

Headlights flash as a car veers up the side road
The blue disco of an ambulance squeals at the junction

A dog left outside alone
sounds scared

Lights dimming along the harbour wall
mark the edge of safety

Wind turbines off the coast are now souls lost in the night
It's getting too black to write

On what part of my body
will the first drop fall?

Coneflower

Echinacea
like Warhol created a
silk-screened daisy

A hyacinth by another name would smell as sweet

These hyacinths aren't tall
though with colour all
are blessed
Lowercinths at best

In drawers that never open

Sunglasses wait in vain to return to fashion
Stray baubles count the days to Christmas

Tangled wires cling to one another
Old birthday cards curl in the dark

Unidentified bits of metal have forgotten their use
A camcorder holds safe untold recordings

Fabric samples chronicle choices unmade
Receipts have grown pale and uninteresting

Toys and board games remember childhood
Shells and curtain rings are now stored litter

Wrapping paper and candles have not lost hope
Biros still have time to leak

Every nation is an immigrant nation

If you believe
in Adam and Eve

then everybody
is a refugee

If you believe in Evolution
you reach the same conclusion

Forget the statue can we just play with the box?

Churchill might find it
an odd tribute
to 'protect' his statue
with a Nazi salute

Brutus's arrival in the land of Albina

Styled after a Syrian daughter
so the legend of Albion is written
until an immigrant from Turkey
changed its name to Britain

The glorious revolution

after being ruled by Romans, Vikings, Danes and the French

Remember when Britain was Great
and Europe left us alone
when we were ruled by the Dutch
before Germans took the throne

British fashion found to be old school

In winter Romans
wore socks and sandals
until run amok
with Goths and Vandals

The common denominator

No number will softly squeeze your hand
No statistic ease your heart
A series of noughts will never understand
what sets your soul apart

You can't calculate the depth of loss
What sum could be enough
to count the tears left unshed
or measure the breadth of love?

My garden is probably past its best

I wonder why I put the word 'probably' in there

I settle a short distance
from the lawn bees

My sun lounger is bust but can suffice
if I alter my weight distribution

A small cabbage-white butterfly
loops back into the sprinkler

Though adding protection against any breeze
the far trees and shrubs are in need of a barber's

Today they're more of a hindrance than a benefit
as the August sun scorches my writing arm

The tall grasses and ornamental thistles
are beginning to look isolated

I've moved my acer to where I can see it better
It stands out like a new filling

My chives have had a fall
Only a faint hint of colour remains on each

like a small bruise
The violets have seen better days

their pollen long gone
they're starting to resemble my grandmother's hair

Five a day I can do in four

I'm told they're good for you
essential for salad and stew
so I make this pledge to eat more veg

but not Courgette – not yet, not even for a bet
Broccoli – not for me
If you plan Lettuce – you can forget us

Beetroot – don't suit
Watercress – does not impress
Butternut Squash – just won't wash

Aubergine – tastes obscene
Kidney, Broad or Mung Bean
Runner, Lima or Split – all taste shit

Sweet Potato or Yam – no thank you mam
Brussels or Alfalfa Sprout – leave it out
Radish tastes baddish

Black Eyed or Chickpeas
I won't be eating any of these
You can include Cucumber in that number

No Parsnips will pass my lips
No Cauliflower in my lunch hour
Artichoke or Asparagus
beyond a joke, do spare us

Celery – doesn't look well on me
Cabbage – does me damage
Garlic – makes me sick

I won't be plumping for Pumpkin
Chard – I find hard
Spinach – just binnage

I'm concentrating on Spuds
and the odd Pea or Carrot
Maybe a variety of Onion
but that's Shallot

A dog's life for a god

Pluto was divine
then a child his name did assign
to one of the ancient spheres

So the planets numbered nine
until we did redefine
this old timer – a minor (after 76 years)

Lodestar

Polaris is only true north
when constellations align

It has shone brighter
and not so bright

and despite Shakespeare
was never constant
despite Spenser
was never steadfast

Earlier generations
were steered by other stars
Future souls
will seek guidance elsewhere

There is no fixed point
in the heavens

It is only that a human life
is so short
and human longing
is so vast

Corona nursery rhymes

i.
One for sorrow
two for joy
three – that's risky at the moment

ii.
Jack be nimble
Jack be quick
stay at home
if you're feeling sick

iii.
Georgie Porgy pudding and pie
kissed the girls
and gave them all the virus

iv.
Ladybird, ladybird fly away home
unless you are out on essential business

v.
Jack and Jill went up the hill
to fetch a pale of water
Did it really need two of them?

vi.
Pease porridge hot, pease porridge cold
pease porridge in the pot five days old
Couldn't we have stockpiled something else?

vii.
Old Mother Hubbard
went to the cupboard
to fetch her poor dog a bone
but when she got there
the cupboard was full of toilet rolls
and tinned soup

viii.
The wheels on the bus
go round and round
but only for essential workers

The shrinking sky

A lifetime ago
the view was different

trees were shorter
my back unbent

only the horizon
edged my vision

Now this old bench
lies overgrown on all sides

wood wrapping my body
like an open coffin

Less hip, more hip replacement

less Michael Stipe more slippers and pipe
less Ramones more aching bones
less Nirvana more bran with sultana
less Linkin Park more blinking in the dark
less AC/DC more feeling queasy
less Sex Pistols more healing crystals
less Iggy Pop more lager top
less Jimmy Hendrix more twin-tub Bendix
less Motörhead more sourdough bread
less Whitesnake more organic wheatflake
less Axl Rose more Waitrose
less Pink Floyd more easily annoyed
less Van Halen more senses failin'
less the Foo Fighters more early nighters
less Kings of Leon more pants with wee on
less Eric Clapton more pants you've …
probably had enough of that poem

Unavoidable neglect

When you find
  a vulnerable child alone
    open to the elements
     ill-equipped
      abandoned
        in the middle of a care system
         there is only one word
          and it is never
           unavoidable

You can take nothing from me
that death hasn't already got its eye on

First I look for straight edges
and corners
then I search out eyes

then faces
then hands
There is solace in making sense of a puzzle

Next I look for lines and patterns
the scarcest shade
the obvious and less obvious features

then pieces that contain more than one colour
or display some detail however small
then those with a change of tone

finally I consider the curved shapes
using trial and error
until eventually the image is complete

It is an exercise in solitude
almost of prayer
irrespective of the final picture

All creatures great and small the Lord God made them all

but no sacred papyrus
prepared us for the Coronavirus

The episcopal water pistol
shows Baptism adaptism

but holy water alone, however clean
can't wash away Covid-19

The sundial casts no shadow

The sky
has had a rough undercoat

A wooden sardine on a stick
swims amongst the chives

Air from Scandinavia
rocks my garden umbrella

Half an orange salmon
hides amongst the terracotta

The hard-to-reach flowers
finally receive a welcome drink

A rusty sparrow
leans ready to swoop

On a neighbour's roof
young gulls whine like babies

A copper tulip dwarfing the lilacs
makes use of its perforations

Driftwood lays
in the shape of driftwood; au natural

A metal cormorant on its heels
hardly guards the gravel

Jazz drumming on my window
the tempo of droplets quickens

Some days the only thing I like deep is my pizza base

Profundity is not for me
I prefer a fun ditty

I'm more convivial with the trivial
not the sort for thought of any import

not woke, just a bloke who likes a joke
I've no pretence to consequence

In touch with how I'm feeling
I fail to find appealing

Mistrusting the meaningful is my MO
I'm callow – so shallow is the way to go

It's too hard to process mindfulness
there's a lot less stress in mindlessness

Making whole the soul is not my goal
the need for purpose is somewhat surplus

I hate to debate on matters of weight
Gravitas can kiss my ass

Worthwhile is not my style
my facile fun's more juvenile

I'm better with breadth than depth
Somewhat akin to Barbie and Ken

So surfing the surface can suffice
like a bimbo in limbo to be precise

A nonchalant dilettante if you want
Egregious, specious and fully facetious

The very gent to experiment with merriment
to train my brain to retain the inane

It'll ever be the brevity of levity
for clever me, whatever be its longevity

Walking through my thoughts I'd bet
you wouldn't even get your ankles wet

Maybe there is another universe where poetry isn't needed

Maybe there's another universe
where I cry your tears
and you cry mine
and we feel joy together

Maybe there's another universe
where at least we try

Let us not bury those merely sleeping

Chilled by a pale blue light
it's easy to believe

that spring will never come
that frost has killed the seeds

that we're lost in the void
forsaken

But even in the darkest night
Earth spins upon its axis

and even in the coldest hour
it moves along its orbit

until we tilt towards the sun
once more

I've no beef with tripe

a Tweet apology to The Tripe Marketing Board for someone on my Twitter feed's use of the word 'tripe' as a derogatory statement

I'm not the type to snipe at tripe
though others find the subject ripe

and some it seems to flummox
my peace pipe I fill with edible stomachs

Under a white flag I send my respects
with no intention to slag or vex

When offered tripe in a bag next
I'll try to curb my gag reflex

The sun navigates a corridor between clouds

The terracing of shingle provides
a platform to view coastal waters

You ease your new swimsuit
into the English Channel

Though intermittently sunkissed
the sea is nearer ice than steam

its distant surface displaying
as airforce camouflage

Afloat in his orange hat
our son resembles a buoy

We raise our eyes
to this gift of open sky

We are making memories
out of the blue

Soon dark giants will edge east
sending a chill

indifferent
to the shadows cast

This poetry is

locally sourced
energy efficient
ethnically resourced
self-sufficient

environmentally friendly
bio-degradable
carbon neutral
fully sustainable

Best before date – on the lid
RRP – ten quid
May contain the word 'nuts'
– just did

I'd sooner be a citizen than a subject

Poet laureate is not my fate
the hereditary potentate is not my mate
I can't relate
I'm more council than country estate

Now please don't miscalculate
to be accurate I would communicate
I bear the royal line no hate
no need for them to abdicate

the work they've done I appreciate
but it's inappropriate they participate
and take on the role as head of state
such position's no longer legitimate

Hereditary privilege is out of date
No child should be born second rate
each day delayed is a day too late
That's something I'd like to articulate

When full equality we can celebrate
and all unfair advantages abate
when laws we create don't discriminate
then Britain could be truly great

and I'll be its loudest advocate
until that date I can wait
and demonstrate and educate
and engage debate

Poet laureate is not my fate
I'll break
           before I bow

The five stages of good grief!

Denial – No, I'd not noticed your haircut

Anger – Who the fuck cut that?

Bargaining – Maybe if you wore a hat

Depression – It's never going to grow back

Acceptance – It's so you

War mongers

If it's prejudice you're supplying
I'm not buying

disquiet you're trading
my interest's fading

vexation you're vending
I'll not be spending

If you're dishing out division
I've made my decision

fear you're floggin'
you're off your noggin

if by spreading alarm
you're hoping for profits
I've got short arms
and deep pockets

Becoming conscious during Covid

Waking but still aching
dream breaking
sleep shaking
senses quaking
comfort forsaking
decision making
future staking
a risky undertaking

Grounded

i.
Whilst engineers discuss tactics
we suck Tic Tacs on the tarmac
The clock tick tocks on their box of tricks
as they try a different tack

ii.
Due to a mundane delay with BA
they say we may not get away
to a fun day this Sunday via the runway
till Monday we may have to stay

iii.
The jet is stuck to the jetty
If we move, it moves as well
We can't cut the umbilical
our 'Stairway to Heaven' is giving us hell

iv.
So, with steps attached to one side
it seems, for now, we're stranded
though, if somehow we manage to fly
they'll come in handy, once we've landed

Those little slices of death

after Edgar Allen Poe

I live to sleep
count endless sheep
drift off deep without a peep

Life is all filler
till you dent a pillow

So get some kip
let eyelids slip
Hypnos worship's where it's hip

Hunker down, be less awake
up-and-about's a big mistake
hit the hay for heaven's sake

Don pyjamas
dream of the Bahamas
chase moonbeams and forget all dramas

Quit your yap
fit that night cap
Fall back in the sack and nap

Perfect slumber's my number one
zeds in bed are second to none

Choose to snooze if you feel dozy
the arms of Morpheus are real cosy

Somnolence – makes perfect sense
let the REMs commence

Never shrink from forty winks
sinking into lengthy blinks
enjoy a rest, a
nice siesta
that's the best advice methinks

Consciousness is overrated
The Sandman's got to be celebrated
I get grisly when I've not hibernated

My circadian clock
is all to cock
time that I was counting flock

Sod reality – that's all behind me
The Land of Nod is where you'll find me

I am not the poet I longed to be

My soul is too thin
though the pain is real enough
it slips from the page

Whisper from a future grave

I'm just earth at this moment
compacted over aeons
fallen plants
and the bodies of creatures past

I'm not yet loosened
hollowed out
defined in rectangles
exposed to sunlight

I'm in no hurry
to embrace more decay
polished oak
laid on my floor

I'm in no hurry
to cover what was once so vital
with the weight of those
long dead

I'm in no hurry
to hold a stone marker
telling of those you loved
and of those who loved you

The secret of eternal youth

To be immortal like the hydra
the path could not be plainer
The organism is literally
a no-brainer

(is it a co-incidence this genus
resembles a penis?)

Chasing immortality

The first Emperor of China
try'na avert his last breath
took mercury which inadvertently
somewhat hastened his death

i. The origin of Nottingham Forest's shirt colour

Garibaldi wore a red shirt
buttoned to the neck
a colour that might cause alert
if guesting on *Star Trek*

ii. Nottingham – first English city of football

To avoid any confusion
remember this little ditty
The City Ground is in the county
the County ground in the city

iii. If blood is red why are veins blue?

Red and White flows through my veins
for blood transfusions please
the only blue veins I entertain
are within the local cheese

iv. Blue cheese for a red

Peter Shilton ate
some Stilton late
despite my dad's advice

He dreamt Forest won the European Cup
woke up
and found they had, twice

In a world without God or fame

There's no
need for a creature
alone
to measure
its stature

When no-one
is looking
what is your nature?

The invisible mantra

Notoriety's not the game for me
My middle name's anonymity
My claim to fame – obscurity

Unavowed by the crowd – I adore it
My world renown – you can ignore it
I'm internationally unknown for it

Looking for kudos
you can exclude us
I'm not even as popular as Judas

You'd hardly rate us as celebrity status
to say I'm in vogue would be to over-inflate us
my moment in the spotlight's more a hiatus

When you're top of the pops
it's hard to pop to the shops
red hot, I'm not – I'll not do swaps

I prefer a flan base to a fan base
It's no disgrace you can't place my face
I like to live my life in lower case

That people ignore me is no ignominy
so Joe Public don't give a fig for me
I'm just happy to have a gig for me

an audience of one is really quite big for me

The unslept

Backwards over my bed
leap uncounted sheep
as the Sandman removes
a single grain of sleep

Converting light into energy

Surrounded by leaves
I sip warm water
flavoured by leaves

the bench underneath me
is made from the trunk
of an oak tree

My son colours leaves
under a green canopy
whilst I write on leaves

my clothes are spun
from plant fibres
my shoes lined with latex

Lavender draws the eye
and all around leaves
soften my world

Without a word spoken
I trade carbon dioxide
for oxygen

On the Revolution of Celestial Spheres
was banned by the Pope after 73 years

Copernicus's ban never chimes
though the church rebukes his crimes
It's hard to reposition the Earth
as the centre of the universe
once it's spun round the sun 73 times

Constantine the Great (or not so)

Constantine legalised Christianity
but with the same breath
ended the life of his wife
and had his son put to death

Next door's cat is nowhere to be seen

Small feathers litter the lawn
The nest in the pergola is empty
My wife had watched it being built
peaked inside to spy the egg
followed the chick grow each day

until today

The cry of a collared dove this morning
now haunts as does the sight of
a mother perched on our window
either come to say goodbye
or perhaps to ask why

Twitter poetry

after Joyce Kilmer

I think that I shall never see
a poem lovely as a tree

on Twitter – paper you don't need
so no tree must die for you to read

Artificial trees

after Joyce Kilmer

I think that I shall never see
a filter lovely as a tree

To make the irony complete
they use wood to make its seat

Ladders of divine ascent

Light tilts from the clouds
like an alien abduction

Snow threatens as smoke rises
from neighbouring roofs

On this ordinary morning
set mostly in monochrome

spot-lit
the sea shines silver

the winter sky
stretches wider

whilst earthbound
I concede to wonder

and dream of angels

An empty hallway awaiting new guests

I've forgotten most of my life
so I wonder what worth it has
if even I
have no memory

The Earth is not a perfect circle

Afternoon sun
strikes the rear of my house
at an oblique angle

the shadow
of an open window
becomes a trapezoid

Seen from the garden
these geometric lines contrast
with the shapes of life

Poppies form a ragtail family
Ornamental thistles
bend with differing curves

Although hundreds of individuals
lavender in the mid-distance
displays as a single unit

This brick façade is regulation
the foliage handcrafted by nature
with little interest in symmetry

No stretch of grass is truly even
Equations underlying a single blade
too complex to calculate

All eyes on the potato

The simple Spud tastes so good
There's none greater than the Tater
This Tuber is uber

King Edward or Jersey Royal
peeled or washed free from soil
ready to fry in oil, bake or boil

Whether you call it Pomme de Terre
or any nom de guerre
to say it will flatter any platter is only fair

I even like Potato Cakes and Patties
Always welcome on my welcome mat is
the aristocrat that is – Tatties

Every Jacket's in the upper bracket
I've never yet met a Croquette that I regret

Dauphinoise or Hasselback
versatility in a sack Spuds never lack
– the power pack snack in the veggie rack

Skins and Crisps have got their glitz
Pomme Frites I love to bits

and though little can eclipse Chips
those French Fries don't take top prize

Neither Crinkle Cut nor Straight
rate as potentate of the plate

Nevertheless they do just edge
the Potato Wedge

The Hash Brown doesn't take the crown
Mash doesn't take the sash

I like Roasties the mosties

The lure of the salmon sandwich

To Seymour Street return I ought t'
swimming upstream against the water
though the 39 bus
is a lot less fuss
and makes the journey shorter

John Byrom

born 29th February 1692, English poet, educator and inventor

Easily confused with Byron
Byrom's distinctive in one way
he died at the age of 71
after only his 17th birthday

Byron trilogy

i. The folly of the Pena Palace, Sintra

In tuk tuk we descend it
on cobbles so thrilling
but I wouldn't recommend it
If you've got a loose filling

ii. Any old Ionian *(bloodletting and illness in Byron's footsteps)*

On an island Ionia
Just north of Kefalonia
Mozzis would not leave me alone here

Romantic Kerkyra its name in Greek
Corfu to you. To be crystal clear
I was bitten 52 times. That's bleak
Once for every week of the year

iii. Epitaph to a dog – Butch not Boatswain

I know
my dog is dead
He can cause no one no harm

even though
my mum had said
he'd gone to live on a farm

Less than temporary

less than temporary
we distract ourselves with vibrations

we fear this is not our home
we wear it like hand-me-downs

we constantly assess the walls
and throw emotions at all obstacles

without a window for escape
we fall tender with this space

What not to say to a poet

I love that poem you did
about the level sands stretching far away

>   That's not mine that's Shelley's
>   Ozymandias

But the one about the nightingale's yours?
>   No, that's Keats

So what was the one you did?
>   I wandered lonely as a cloud

Isn't that Wordsworth?
>   Yes, I am Wordsworth

Right, then I'll have a copy of
The Ancient Mariner

>   Certainly,
>   would you like me to sign it

>   from Lord Byron?

Catchy verse

Coronavirus
trying to expire us
you're not a bug
I find desirous

Fly-solation

I saw a fly today
land on my welcome mat
I was happy I must say
for such company as that

A martyr to my 'John the Baptist complex' I lose my head

These are the clothes I will wear when I'm dead
This camel hair suits me fine
it sort of tickles

I know those that come after
will exceed in every way
This is as it should be

I have had my fill of locusts and wild honey
I have seen the spirit descend
We're all in the wilderness making straight the path

You who are made alive
anoint yourself with water
Herald a new grace

You are harbingers of purity
You are Elijah
Bear witness

Those that come after will be the lamb
Those that come after
will light the seven heavens

Rather than ride to the third Crusade
in Nottingham Richard should have stayed
and had himself a 'swift lemonade'

Only one 'Trip to Jerusalem'
should he have bin conciderin'
then the Salutation and then the Bell Inn
Top that with a curry
home in a taxi
that's what I call a win win

No point in getting Saladin
it'll only go off

i. 1642 – a poem for GCSE syllabus

Answering only to God
Charles sought to save his crown
he raised his standard in Nottingham
and God blew the bastard down

ii. Cast irony

Little John strikes the deepest note
timely every hour
reminding us that outlaws exist
in the very heart of power

iii. Is Helen elsewhere in Nottingham?

Menelaus and Agamemnon
addressed love lost in the night
I make a stand mid Joseph's lions
lest I mix up left from right

A day off from social media

Birdsong seems to have increased in volume
I can't help but smell the wildest of roses

My joints feel a little rheumatic
but not enough to warrant complaint

The memory of green tea
lingers somewhere between throat and brain

The reflection from the edge of cloud hurts
like I'm staring too close to a computer screen

I could close my eyes with very little effort
and no harm would befall the world

I'm not good at self-deprecation

I've fallen out of hate
with myself of late
No more do I gnaw at my core
nor abhor each character flaw
There's time for self-loathing
when you're decomposing

Now beating myself up
is not a cup from which I sup
To get my own goat
don't float my boat
                          I'm
not giving myself a hard time
On matters self-critical
my chatter's apolitical

It's unwise to self-despise
to manifest a detest at doing your best
I've no compulsion for self-repulsion
no judgement to be repugnant
no animosity in my verbosity
no facility for hostility towards my ability

I'm happy with the entity 'me'
to be this identity you see

I've made an amigo of my ego
Ergo – negativity I simply torpedo

I've no bone to pick, nor a boner
about my own homegrown persona
a nonstarter as a martyr
I'm persona grata

The origin of Old Coach Road, Wollaton

Gladly remembered as the great grandfather of rail
Most of his ventures did so badly fail
That Huntingdon Beaumont died sadly in gaol

A tram named after him would surely be fitting
Having pioneered the rails on which they are sitting
Though admittedly for horses with a great deal more shitting

Nottingham tram trilogy

i. Mad, bad and safe for passengers

If Byron's name upon a tram
you see amid your trails
be assured unlike the man
it won't go off the rails

ii. She walks in beauty like the night tram

She walks in beauty like the night
of cloudless climes and starry skies
If from the tram she did alight
she'd be at home now eating pies

iii. Loneliness of the long distance on runners

If I am
to be hit by a tram

by Alan Sillitoe
I'd plan to go

Pearly Gates via Tram Two-One-Nine
walking slowly to the finish line

It lives!

I blame you
it's your fault
without you
this poem
is not
brought
to life

I
merely
put
some
used
parts
together

You are
the real
Dr Frank
enstein
infusing life
into the
being

There are no peacocks beneath this tired sky

Chasing murder
under the chestnut tree
a small ginger boy zigzags
in a fluorescent tee-shirt

I pay to sit still
dull brown and green
blurring the bottom half
of my windscreen

Exhaustion overrides eyelids
as darkness juts its neck
Blood soup drugs me
like a welcome fever

A pied piper casts his spell
and all along the barred fence
crotchets and semiquavers
dance the score

Good form

I adore a ditty or the odd clerihew
I love a comic limerick too
They work fine
most of the time
though for a funeral they seldom do

Acrostic poem

A
C urious
R use
O f
S orts
T o
I nterest
C *nts

Fare thee well

Time to go
so cheerio
don your chapeau
and blow

Take a hike
get on your bike
hasta la vista
see ya mister
pick any exit you like

Make your excuse
hitch your caboose
bon voyage
time to vamoose

ta-ta, toodle-oo
sayonara, adieu
Ciao, take a bow
bugger off now

Be gone
do one
I wouldn't go as far
as to say au revoir

nor TTFN
nor auf wiedersehen

And so that you're sure
and to avoid any doubt
don't let the door
hit you on the way out

The Christmas star in a time of darkness

Some look to Heaven for a sign
where gods reflect the light
where time, space and hope align
to consecrate the night

The poetry unwritten

My son isn't yet able to articulate
many of his feelings in words
He doesn't have the vocabulary
That's not to say
he doesn't have the emotions

I too have emotions for which
I don't have suitable words
and sometimes
feelings about which
I've no desire to communicate

My time
within this sunlit garden
may be no greater
for me writing this to you
but still

here today
I express myself
and communicate
          though
not everything

Way before the dawn of man
1,200,000,000 years ago – sex began

If fossil evidence can be believed
the single-celled Eukaryote was much relieved

It's either them or Ribonucleic Acid (RNA)
that deserve congratulation
for inventing sex
and replacing masturbation

Reincarnation's not been kind to me
I'm history's greatest back seat driver
I've never quite fulfilled my destiny
I'm about as famous as Lord Godiva

I used to scrump apples from Isaac Newton
I was usher at the Tower of Babel
I tried to sell Rip Van Winkle a futon
I was head of Catherine the Great's stable

I dry cleaned Sir Walter Raleigh's cape
I was Samson's regular barber
I lost at bowls to Sir Francis Drake
I was the look out at Pearl Harbour

I was Ivan the Terrible's court jester
I gave Lord Wellington the boot
I was Socrates' food tester
I rented the deckchair to King Canute

I was city architect for Jericho
I was Odysseus' map reader
I was a music teacher to Nero
I was Barabbas's cheer leader

I've never quite made it in any of my lives
I'm more a shed than a treasure trove
I was bridesmaid to all of Henry VIII's wives
and now I'm Michael Gove

A tree with its own visitors' centre

When I was but a wee kid
in the Major Oak tree we hid
like Robin Hood
up to no good
avoiding the parking fee – three quid

Batman filmed at Wollaton Hall missed the main attraction

The Dark Knight Rises
is a cracking brooding thriller
but Wayne Manor's mood did suffer from
the lack of a stuffed gorilla

12,000 year old Frank (Capra ibex) from Creswell Crags, Notts

the only cave painting to be defaced by graffiti

Though the artist has long since disappeared
his genius remains to be revered
On this ancient deer for all to be shared
he added his initials and a little beard

Fifteen ways to leave your lockdown

Get the vaccine, Maxine
Get the Pfizer, Eliza
Get your shot, Dot
before you cannot

Get your jabs, Babs
Get AstraZeneca, Anneka
Inoculate, Kate
don't hesitate

Get Johnson & Johnson, Bronson
Get it in your vein, Lorraine
Immunize, Guys
pay no attention to lies

Get the Moderna, Verner
Get it in your capillary, Hillary
It's just a prick, Mick
so don't get sick

Curtail the virus, Cyrus
Stop the disease, Louise
Vaccinate, Nate
before it's too late

Responsibility wakes me

At its weakest
the dawn still dilutes
the darkness

Gold seeps
over the far corner
of the sea

Already in flight
birds circle
as yet silhouettes

The wind complains
to the glass
like an insistent ghost

Higher stratus clouds above the channel

It is trying to snow
on the sea

Grey and silver
hoping for white

The flakes are so fine
they curl on the breeze

too near rain
to settle

Waves appear
like creases on paper

whilst shadows sail
across the teased surface

off the coast a lone dredger
ignores the weather

Droplets hang like jewels
on my Juliet balcony

From behind my window
I watch the circling of water

as gas, solid and liquid

Shaking hands with Elvis *(or wearing a wooden onesie)*

If there's one thing you can trust
each one of us will bite the dust
go belly up and go bust
join the just and the unjust

Kick the can
pay the ferryman

Buy the farm
lose our charm

Go West
put on a pine vest

Snooze under the soil
shuffle off this mortal coil

Come to terms
count the worms

Croak, choke
go up in smoke
become an ex-gal
or an ex-bloke

Greet the Grim Reaper
become a late sleeper

Disappear from the map
take a dirt nap

Fall off our perch
Spend half a day at church

Lose the lifeforce
ride the pale horse

Take that last bus
become posthumous

Cross the river Styx
snuff out the candlesticks
check into the Motel Deep 6

Pop our clogs
meet Hades' dogs

Melt into the mass
lie on the wrong side of the grass

Kick the bucket
tell life to fuck it

Give up the ghost
become toast

Be gone for a Burton
pass through the curtain

Cash in our chips
pucker our lips
kiss our ass goodbye
and die

Our final form filled in
Elvis has left the buildin'

Boudica is a thing of the pasta

I'm off to Colchester
where despite the Iceni
you can still ingest a
homemade tortellini

T' realism

L.S. Lowry painted under Salford skies
landscapes of tender gloom
and northern portraits so good the pies
seem to follow you round the room

Happy St. David's Day

On St. David's Day in Cardiff
I eat Welsh cakes by the ton
They look and taste as if
a pancake's made love to a scone

Surface water in the marina
reflects a green far darker
than the open sea

Fishing boats and yachts
sleep with their masts erect
like a giant bed of nails

Only the weight of the moon
and the circulation of air
stir the channel

Birds perch on aerials
rusting satellite dishes
and unused chimneys

Walkways are strangely still
like a Lowry painting
with no people

The only two words
visible on the harbour wall
are DEAD and SLOW

We have a statue to an outlaw
who may not even be real
At the National Ice Centre
a whirligig of steel

A bronze statue to 'Shoppers'
adorning Chapel Bar
Queen Victoria on her Embankment
if you want to go that far

A weird Chorus Line
at the top of Maid Marian Way
A mirror outside the playhouse
if you don't want to see the play

The 'Circle of Life' at QMC
A big hand called 'Healing Energy'
An ice cream cone at the university
taller than the Statue of Liberty

A signpost outside the Flying Horse
one in Houndsgate too
If that's not obscure enough
there's a Mammoth at NTU

A steel dragon in Sneighton
A statue of William Booth
along with another of Bendigo
perched on a pub roof

George the Beekeeper in Beeston
A 'Waterhead' with no spring
at the East Midland conference centre
a big thermometer looking thing

A bust of Jesse Boot
A green man made of wood
A war memorial called 'Hope'
A metal heron in West Bridgford

Byron's Bust at the castle
On King Street Brian Clough
People in the Arboretum
I've never even heard of

Holding a little blue flower
Lawrence at the Uni
A sculpture tree in the lace market
like Nottingham needs another tree

Statues to Prosperity, Commerce, Law
and one to Knowledge, though
still no statue it seems
to Alan Sillitoe

Is this how we treat
one of our own?
Else's Lions would weep
were they not made of stone

It's

only the number
of beats to the human heart
that makes it finite

Folding

A corner in each hand
we shake the sheet

Place edges together
and repeat

Move towards each other
till both ends meet

A domestic dance
for hands and feet

A meditation
making bedding neat

A chore but more
a ritual treat

A task shared
perhaps bittersweet

Stick or twist again like we didn't last summer?

It is almost a year since you
stood under a different roof
over a year since you sat under one

I've examined the dentist's ceiling
entered the post office and the bank
masked

There are only three days a week now
bin day, delivery day
and all others

Our meals, clothes and jigsaws,
are on a rota system
shaving optional

Our stomachs have expanded
with compensation and diversion
Quality control now Quality Street

We spin through the news cycle
on our exercise bikes
repetition being the new variant

Our schedule –
a vitamin blister
like a healthy advent calendar

Daffodils alert us
once again
winter is receding

Crocuses brave
the possibility
of late frost

We are fed numbers
when what we remember
are names

How are we to celebrate
these anniversaries
of Corona?

To the night

If I lose the stars in static
if I feast too full to breathe
if I bleach into the dayscape
if I flail in darkened seas

if I choke upon this chaos
if I paint the sky unkind
if I skive from those I've loved
if the stillness in me dies

if I ever forget the moon
save me

The eleventh month is named after the number nine

I'm never sure when autumn
becomes winter
Nature has its own calendar

Sunlight hits the sea
through a gap in the clouds
like heartburn on the chest

the reflection so bright
when my eyes look down
all focus is lost

The sun is still as hot
as it was in summer
it is us that are leaning away

F.O.P. (but not ready to drop)

today I'm retro
not dead yet though
old school
easy to ridicule
an old codger
a coffin dodger
a walking fossil
my age – colossal
over the hill
landfill
but here still
and hard to kill

a has-been
but evergreen
retired
but not expired
decrepit
not ready to quit
a crone
but not quite prone
vintage
almost out-of-print age
infirm
but going full term

heading for the sunset
not done with the fun yet
golden
still able to hold on
time tested
but not yet bested
experience-rich
not dead in a ditch
feeling my age
not leaving the stage
on the slippery slope
but not without hope

The distance between clouds

I have very little I can say to you my friend

I can only offer a gentle reminder
        to listen to your child
look upon the face of the sea
                        in all weathers
and put your arms
                around those you love

very little
        but everything